Teaching Life's Lessons to the Youth

Book 3

Teens in Conflict

B.Y. Stuart, DRS PhD LCPC

I'll get him/her if it is the last thing I do

Do not become so angry that you go to bed
planning to do harm
to someone.

Be ye angry, and sin not:
let not the sun go down upon your wrath:

(Ephesians 4:26)

———————————

Let's *Identify* the problem!

Let's *Face* it!

Let's get **to the *Root* of it!**

Let's *Discuss* it!

It is time to *Resolve* it!

Let us pray for guidance (Luke 18:1).

Teaching Life's Lessons to the Youth Book 3
Teens in Conflict

Library of Congress Control Number: 2019908947

ISBN 13:978-1466409033

Be ye angry, and sin not: let not the sun go down upon your wrath:

Neither give place to the devil.

Ephesians 4:26-27

Table of Contents

Teens in Conflict

There are young adults who are extremely angry, and whose behaviours are often violent and destructive. They are angry about many things for which they need an outlet to vent their feelings. In many cases, they are looking for role models and cannot find someone who is trustworthy both inside and outside of the church. The need for expression makes them spew their emotions on anyone who is available – parents, siblings, friends, and the public; or anyone who is in close contact.

Frequently, this anger could be the result of exposure to violence in the home, family problems, unrest in the society from both governmental and political arenas, disappointments, school situations, and other circumstances that are community, religious, or of national origin.

Beginning from the home, in some of those settings there are destructive conditions that are harmful to the teen. Some parents do not express sincere love or time to listen to their children. They believe that gifts will replace the most important necessities such as love, attention, nurturing, acknowledgement, and human expressions, which make life reasonably comfortable. They do not spend time with or talk with their children.

Those young minds struggle with a vast array of negatives, failures, and frustrations, which occur around them and even in their own lives. In the home, they may face poverty, parents who are on drugs, domestic abuses, and such like. Conditions, which make life difficult and almost impossible for them to cope. The teens become distraught, and aimless without hope and purpose wondering how they will ever fit into the milieu of life-changing circumstances facing them every day.

Teens often take matters into their own hands because adults have failed them. They are disappointed and feel neglected with the belief that everyone forgets them. Their perception is that no one cares about their welfare. Therefore, anger is the only expression for their dissatisfaction.

It takes a concerned individual to recognize and understand the distress faced by teens. That insightful person might reach out to capture those who are walking into traps that might ensnare them for life.

Teens in Conflict, is a resource book with techniques specifically for teaching teens and young adults non-violence response when dealing with conflict situations. It gives reasons why teens should learn inoffensive methods for managing conflicts in their lives.

Teens in Conflict, is an ideal resource for any adult who works with teens and young adults to help them reach out to those who are at risk, and others already in trouble.

Suggestions for Teaching

Teens in Conflict, is for teaching Conflict Management skills to teenagers and young adults.

The recommended suggestions give the teacher a wide scope for teaching teens alternative methods for managing difficult situations.

Each teacher should improvise on these techniques with suitable ideas for the needs of the students.

Do research on world leaders who used non-violent principles courageously and successfully for a better world.

Set the students up in groups to role play the behaviours of those persons who have changed society, and their own nations with the use of non-violent methods.

By bringing each lesson to life, every student should derive the best learning experience possible that will help to change old methods of managing conflicts, and learn new skills for managing difficult emotional experiences.

Teachers may use any or a combination of the following methods:

1. Role plays
2. Simulations
3. Set up groups in opposing situations, and so on.

4. Be creative, and allow students to be
    a. Critical,
    b. Innovative,
    c. Resourceful, and
    d. Analytical.

5. In some situations, ask "What if...?" in devising other options, for reaching amicable solutions to problems.

About the Author

Dr. Barbara Stuart is a Licensed Pastoral Counsellor and Ordained Minister. The call to write has given her a sincere love for sharing this gift from God through the number of books she has written.

Teaching Life's Lessons to the Youth is the third book in the series of three.

Dr. Stuart developed her love for teens when she taught high school after leaving the nursing profession. The years spent as a certified teacher, prompted her to do more to help teens face life's struggles.

Having brought up two sons, gave her insight on how to tread into this territory with the constant guidance of the Holy Spirit.

She is a Christian Educator, and Licensed Pastoral Counsellor. Dr. Stuart is Founder of Faith Restoration Ministries International [FRMI] & Shekinah Theological College [STC] Inc. www.frministry.org

Keep thy heart with all diligence;

for out of it (are) the issues of life.

Proverbs 4:23

Objectives

With so many economic, social, and other presenting problems, the presence of anger among people including teens is out of control. Sometimes it is difficult finding the right things to say, because someone seems ready for a fight.

A slight glance at another may result in a harsh *"What are you looking at?"* The response might be *"You are nothing to look at."* An insignificant remark may lead to something destructive.

For these reasons and more, teens need a course in conflict management skills. It will teach them that the type of character displayed is what others will use to judge them.

Therefore, they should behave in a manner that will cause others to respect them.

The instructions and exercises will help them learn how to control emotions, build suitable character, develop positive leadership and social skills, and to deal with interpersonal problems when they occur.

At the end of the program, students will be able to:

1.   Identify and describe dynamics that might result in conflict;

2.   Recognize the role of perceptions and realities;

3.   Identify differences between assertiveness and aggressiveness;

4.   Develop interpersonal skills to build positive character, and improved relationships;

5.   Improve communication skills of listening, empathizing, questioning, and reflecting;

6.   Deal with emotions such as anger;

7.   Develop leadership skills;

8.   Understand and analyze conflict situations, and deal with them constructively;

9.   Brainstorm multiple solutions for problems to reach win-win solutions.

1

What is Conflict

We can describe conflict as any disagreement between individuals [*interpersonal*], within groups [*intra-group*] or within it begin in an individual [*intra-psychic* which often leads to dissonance]. A Conflict does not begin without a reason or cause. There is always an antecedent [event], which activates emotion evoking a response that might be negative to cause conflict to occur. This begins with cognitive assessment of an event. Depending on the outcome of the evaluation, it may result in a reaction or response.

The course of a conflict is systematic because it begins with a precursor [event], such as a slight encounter, a misunderstanding, disrespect of personal values or anything which causes someone to be annoyed or upset. The response exhibited will either build or hurt the person's character or relationship with others. It is not so much what or who caused hurt. What is most important is how the injured person responds to the preceding event [a slur], which depends on the outcome of the evaluation of that situation.

Nevertheless, the perceptions of an individual after a violation of personal values, beliefs, and opinions may affect attitude and behaviour. This depends on the type of emotion elicited from the event. An innocent remark can be the cause of a conflict situation. Moreover, conflict does not need any particular place or time to occur. Similar to fire which needs oxygen and fuel; conflict needs people who are frustrated, with differences of opinions, and who have needs. Nothing happens of itself.

There is always cause and effect. Any insensitive remark or action will make people demonstrate volatile *emotions* of anger to affect themselves, and others.

Scenario:

Jackie and *Colleen* are classmates. They are on casual speaking terms; but not friendly. One day *Colleen* whispered to her neighbour, "I like *Jackie's* new 'do'," meaning the new hairstyle.

Unfortunately, *Jackie* happened to glance around just in time to see the smiles on the girls' faces and mistook this negatively. She in turn gave them a nasty look in response.

At the end of school that day, *Jackie* confronted *Colleen* and her friend with a barrage of unkind words. They were shocked and wondered the reason for the assault.

Finally, *Jackie* calmed down and the girls told her about the kind remark they made about her hairstyle.

Here is an example how easily a misunderstanding can cause problems and disagreement. In the situation above, it is clear to see there was an *interpersonal* problem that could have created animosities and hostilities if the matter were not resolved.

Next, we can view conflict from three categories. These include the way we *perceive* and *evaluate* an event; the way it *affects* our *feelings* and how we *respond* to the event; and how we *behave* in *response* to an event. Consequently, we are looking at perception [*cognition*], feelings [*affective*], and action [*behaviour*].

With the incident above, Jackie took the situation with Colleen and the other girl personally. From her *perception*, they were being unkind, and her *feelings* were hurt. At the end of the day, she took *action*.

Additionally, it does not matter who we are, or how highly spiritual or educated we might be, we will face conflicts all the time. These might be in the form of disagreements to likes and dislikes, poor communication, personal needs and failures, different values and beliefs, unsociable behaviours, and a host of other situations that we find disagreeable, and which make us angry.

Those circumstances can cause us to behave out of control due to misunderstanding about a communication or an event. For this reason, perceptions play a major role on how we respond to conflicts.

Regardless of how violated we may feel, each person must keep in mind that the things we do and the way we behave follow us wherever we go. Whatever our position in life, there is someone who will recognize us somewhere. This should make everyone who wants to leave positive examples, to display commendable behaviours for others to follow.

Nevertheless, despite our feelings about conflicts and the things which cause distress, conflicts of themselves are harmless. What makes conflicts destructive is the way we manage or cope with the events which cause them.

Discussion

1. What is conflict? Describe any situation which made you angry.

2. What are the different types of conflicts, and how is conflict categorized? Give an example of each and explain how the incident could be dealt with.

3. Do you think Colleen behaved appropriately in whispering to her friend even though she meant no harm? What could she have done differently?

4. Do you think Jackie acted properly? Should she have asked why Colleen smiled at her before taking offense?

5.   If you were hurt by someone, and did not inform the individual, but internalized your feelings, what kind of conflict is this?

6.   What are some outcomes for interpersonal conflicts? Refer to your own experience.

7.   How can the way we manage conflicts affect our character and relationships?

8.   How important is our character to interpersonal relationships?

9.   How could the outcome in the exercise above have been different?

10.   How would you advise each person in the situation?

2

Why Learn Conflict Management

Conflict management teaches a non-violent method for resolving disputes. It makes disputants *think, analyze, discuss,* and *devise options* for *decisions* for effective outcomes and to improve relationships. Students who learn conflict management skills are in a better position to establish an environment which is conducive for learning, and for effective interpersonal interactions. Disputes occur when people interact closely with each other such as in the home, church, social group, or school. Therefore, a model of conflict management in the curricula will help students develop a more constructive practical learning experience to deal with differences of opinions when they occur in their interactions with teachers and their peers.

Undoubtedly, the teaching of conflict management concepts will present a model for dealing with incidents in the school for both students and teachers. The knowledge and application of this technique influence students to determine how they should respond to the dynamics of conflict. The course teaches them to think wisely before responding (Philippians 4: 8); and to control their emotions which play a significant role in the escalation of conflicts. Both the school and church are ideal settings and more advantageous for teaching conflict management skills to the youth. These are environments where teens are prepared spiritually and intellectually for the next level in life.

Within the various programs offered, some students learn leadership skills that will advance them into responsible positions when they leave school. The major significance for learning these skills means that a conflict management program will serve even a greater purpose, since it would facilitate in their development and widen their understanding of successful leadership abilities.

Indisputably, it is in the school environment where they often have violent encounters with other students resulting in painful outcomes from some situations. Those incidents take place on the school bus, in the classroom, bathrooms, and other places. Teaching students non-violent conflict resolution skills will make them better able to cope with peer pressure, and other situations that can lead them into trouble. Students build positive character as they learn alternative methods for managing disputes and various problems.

In addition, knowledge of conflict management helps students to display effective social behaviours among one another. They display these attitudes by being polite in their interactions, while they learn to restrain themselves even when pushed to the limit. In such a situation, there will still be that sense of concern for consequences for destructive behaviours. There will be the absence of selfishness in the classroom as each one seeks to help the other for the improvement, advancement, and success of the group. Cultural, religious, and personal differences can then be resolved to bring about patience, acceptance, respect, and open-mindedness for each other.

Effective conflict management skills can produce outcomes to strengthen relationships, act as a catalyst for change in one's thoughts, and enhance the development of successful problem solving and decision-making skills. Through this program, students also learn active critical thinking skills in terms of deductive reasoning to form inferences and arrive at conclusions. This type of activity creates an exercise in creative problem solving skills to result in a higher quality of management when in a leadership position.

Furthermore, the ability to deal with conflict in a constructive manner is one of the major interpersonal social skills for the youth to acquire. It will help them to develop constructive dispute resolution expertise that will benefit them as they proceed on *the road of life*.

Therefore, this learning awareness is necessary in any teaching environment; and as potential leaders, it is vital that students know how to manage problems constructively. It helps them to demonstrate positive behaviours in the home and community at large. Their scope in knowledge will expand as they learn to use skills such as effective listening and reflecting, rather than being impulsive with their emotions.

3

An Overview of Conflict

Conflict is a systematic process, which usually begins with one person who is angry or distressed about some type of issue. I believe that it would be safe to say that so long as someone else is involved, it is <u>social conflict</u>. While internal conflict is with the self. That person may act out on impulse, or internalize the situation and processes it with negative thoughts. Whether in haste or on reflection, it is from the evaluation of the process which will result in conflict outcomes. When this situation occurs, the result can be either destructive or constructive. Frequently, it only takes a slight miscommunication or misunderstanding between individuals or group to bring about disagreement, even between close friends or relatives.

Maria and *Jim* were in a meeting planning the Sunday School outing. Jim made a remark, which Maria thought was out of context. On reflection, she felt embarrassed and left the meeting in a hurry without making a comment. Later, *Acton,* who was present at the meeting, saw her and asked why she left in such a hurry. *Maria* explained that *Jim* had insulted her by the remark which he made. *Acton* immediately explained that the remark was not against her; but an innocent illustration concerning the topic of discussion.

According to *Maria, Jim* looked in her direction when he made the negative remark, which was really the last portion of the statement he made. What she did not know was that he expected a response from her, but she misunderstood him, and took it personally. Evidently, *Maria* completely missed the full statement because according to her, she was not paying attention in the meeting, but was only present in body. She responded to what *she heard,* and walked out of the meeting with all eyes on her.

In the case with *Maria*, her lack of attention in the meeting resulted in misunderstanding, followed by her inappropriate response for walking out in anger. She evaluated what she heard, and thought *Jim* was referring to her. She did not take the initiative to ask *what* the statement was about, and whether it was really meant to cause her distress.

If *Acton* had not intervened and explained the situation, the presence of conflict in the group would cause stress, tension, and frustration for everyone the next time they met. Clearly, there was evidence of misunderstanding, and her evaluation of what she heard caused *Maria* to take action by leaving the meeting with resentment against *Jim*. Her inaccurate assessment of the incident made her respond according to her *thoughts* about being insulted, and the emotion of *embarrassment*, which led to the decision to walk out [*behaviour*] without an explanation.

Regardless of the cause for a dispute, conflict of itself is an inevitable natural course of event that takes place daily in the lives of people who closely interact with one another. Nonetheless, whatever the context: whether personal, in the home, at the workplace, church, college, or in a group, no one should ignore the presence of conflict. When this happens, it might escalate into other serious problems. However, a conflict does not *always* have to escalate out of control when it occurs. The *response* to an event depends on the effect of a <u>presumed</u> or <u>deliberate</u> violation, and the *perception* of the one offended. What makes conflict seems objectionable is the way it is managed.

Some individuals are gentle at coping with conflicts and will withdraw or ignore its existence [*escape*]. This response may work for a while, but there is no guarantee that the dispute will go away. In another situation, the person might [*compromise* or *accommodate*] insults and wrongs from others because the individual wants to maintain a relationship. This position is destructive to everyone.

Nevertheless, when conflict is managed in an environment with a warm atmosphere with who people who listen to each other, and talk about their differences [*collaboration*], it is the most effective and appropriate method. In such a setting, effective outcomes can result (Matthew 18: 15).

Discussions on the foregoing two Chapters

1. Ask students to list and discuss the benefits of learning conflict management.
2. How can the acquisition of conflict management skills help students to be future successful leaders?
3. How can knowledge of conflict management help when there are cultural and other differences?
4. In what other ways can a conflict management model help to prevent non-violence?
5. What are some of the places violence can erupt in the school community?
1. Ask the students to relate a conflict event when the situation got out of hand because of misunderstanding.
2. How important is effective listening and being present in a conversation? Ask for explanations.
3. Should Maria have walked out of the meeting the way she did? What could she have done differently?
4. What role did Acton play in the outcome? Would you have acted as he did or considered it none of your business?
5. From the scene above, what were some of the causes for the conflict with Maria?
6. What are some ways in which people respond to conflict?

One moment of caution is better

than a *lifetime*

of sorrow!

4

Conflict is Systematic

Sateene and Dorlee have been best friends since they were in grade school.
They are now both high school seniors.

A conflict situation begins with an offence [*event*] when at least one person feels disrespected or hurt. The person thinks about the offence [*cognitive process*], and evaluates to decide how to resolve the emergent feelings [*emotions*] from the assessment of the incident. The outcome may result in a physical attack [*action/behaviour*], or an emotional expression of anger. Let us follow the illustration below.

1. *Event*

Friday evening, *Sateene* received a text message from *Dorlee* asking for the two of them to meet at the mall Saturday at 10:00 am. She arrived at 9:30 all excited because they were going to shop for a new outfit. However, after waiting an hour, *Dorlee* did not arrive. *Sateene* became agitated and hurriedly sent her friend a text message; but there was no response. She waited two hours, still *Dorlee* did not turn up. *Sateene* was both concerned and upset with her friend for not calling. Eventually, she left the mall very angrily and disappointed, blaming *Dorlee* who did not keep her promise. On her way home, *Sateene* called her friend several times, still no response.

At one time, she became concerned about her, but quickly brushed the thought aside. This was not the first time that *Dorlee* had turned up late after making plans to meet. This time she did not turn up, and could not be reached by phone.

2. Cognitive *Process*

Decision

Later, *Sateene* thought that although *Dorlee* was usually late, this behaviour was unlike her. She pondered about the relationship, and concluded that the friendship did not deserve any form of disrespect. What made matters worse was that she had tried to reach *Dorlee* several times, but each time the message went to voice mail. She did not even respond to the text messages.

Sateene decided she would not give *Dorlee* another chance, and she wanted the friendship ended. This time she would not accept any apology from *Dorlee*. This friendship is over!

3. Emotions

Feelings

On the way home, *Sateene* became extremely angry and grew worse by the minute. She was fuming. Finally, she called *Dorlee* again in frustration leaving a nasty message for her. After not receiving a response, she turned off her phone and went home in a rage. She banged her room door shut in anger for being stood up by her friend. She was embarrassed and avoided her mother's concern and questioning gaze.

4. Behaviour

Confrontation

Later that morning, *Dorlee* went to *Sateene's* home, whose mother answered the door. She knocked on her friend's door, but no answer came. She continued to wait and called out her name, but *Sateene* was adamant and refused to answer. From behind the door, *Sateene* told *Dorlee* that she was "inconsiderate, rude, and selfish. This time the relationship is over." However, *Dorlee* ignored her ranting and told her that there was an accident on the road, which held up the traffic for two hours, and she had left her phone at home. *Dorlee* asked forgiveness and for another chance at their long friendship.

Think about the following:

1. Why was Sateene so upset with Dorlee? Do you think that since they were friends for so long, she should have been so angry?
2. Should she give her friend another chance?
3. What would you have done?
4. Why should we not assume the reasons for another person's action when we do not know the circumstances as in the case with these two friends?
5. There was a situation which was beyond the control of Dorlee which caused her to be late.
   a. What have you learned from this incident?
   b. What do you learn about judging and misunderstanding?

Discussion

1. Describe the different conflicts in this event, for example *interpersonal, intra-psychic*. Explain your answer pointing our specific examples.
2. How can this conflict escalate into greater problems?
3. In the story above, describe evidence of perception, misunderstanding and misinterpretation of behaviour, emotions, cognitive process, and behaviours.
4. Is it wrong to be angry? Explain.
5. How does anger affect a relationship?

6. If you were in Sateene's place, how would you have handled the situation?

7. Explain your feelings at that critical moment when you could not hear from your friend. What are some of the emotions that would be evident?

8. How would you have behaved, and what actions would you have taken when your friend did not turn up or answered her phone? It was not the first time she had been late.

5

Some Causes for Conflict

Similar to all other situations, conflict does not come from out of the air; there are many reasons which cause it to occur. The offended person may speak out in anger or do the wrong thing to the wrong person who had nothing to do with the situation. Below are some situations that will cause conflict, leading to anger if the situation gets out of control.

Poor Communication Skills

Communication is the normal way in which we interact with each other. We do this through words, symbols, gestures, and body language. Despite the medium used, the recipient must understand the message for it to be effective, and there must be a response for it to be complete. When a problem arises in a relationship this could be the result of misunderstanding or miscommunication. Evidence could be in the type of message, language or medium used, tone, time received, the interpretation, or response to the message. Sometimes the language is offensive to the receiver to cause distress and hostility.

Differences of Opinions

Conflict can begin with an argument or disagreement when one person becomes emotional about beliefs, values, opinions, ideas, or perception. There is nothing wrong with having different views, but the individual must not expect everyone to accept his or her perspectives. If there is respect for each other, there will be fewer opportunities for conflicts to occur. However, when there is lack of emotional control, a simple argument can cause disputants to become angry because of a hurtful exchange.

Joni and *Claris*.

During a class debate, *Joni* commented that people from a certain geographical region were always noisy. *Claris* opposed her stating that everyone makes noises, and she should not label all the people from that area in one category. The argument went on with hurtful remarks to each other. It became very loud until they were at the point of being physical before the teacher regained order. (*Discuss this situation*).

Cultural Differences

Since people travel from one place to the other, there is every reason why cultural conflicts will develop in school, the workplace, church or anywhere they meet and interact. One main reason with this type of conflict is that what is acceptable in one cultural setting may not be suitable in another.

Carlton comes from a family where it was not unusual to live at home until you were married. His girlfriend Karen's parents set her up in an apartment at 18 years of age. She could not understand why Carlton lived at home at the age of 22 years.

This became a constant battle for them. Moreover, his parents insisted on the two of them remaining in the living room when *Karen* visits. Obviously, *Karen* is not used to this type of parental interference. According to her, *Carlton* has one week to make a decision if he wants to be with her. (*What are your opinions?*).

Interpersonal Relationships

The assumption is that ineffective interpersonal relationship is one of the major sources for conflict to occur. This happens when an individual wants to satisfy a need regardless of how this might affect others. [*Resolve the situation below*].

Pauline, who is 16, shares a room with her 12 year-old sister *Cheryl*. Although they love each other, they are always bickering due to the little-sister, big-sister syndrome.

The problem is that *Cheryl* uses *Pauline's* personal things and does not return them to their rightful place. *Pauline's* weakness is that she is very messy and expects her sister to clean up after her. Several times, they were 99.9% close to blows; but mom always intervened. *How would you resolve this problem*?

Judging one another

One of the weaknesses we often display is judging an event without first obtaining the facts. This happens frequently, and it takes someone who is very perceptive to withhold judgment until all the facts are presented. This is where critical thinking skills are very important. To judge a situation without first obtaining all the information about an incident is to assume, and then pronounce sentence against an individual or a situation. Critical thinking to assess conflict is one of the most effective methods for conflict management, which will allay fears about an event when the facts are brought together and examined. From the accumulation, and assessment of those facts deductions are made to arrive at an answer to reach a successful resolution.

Discussion

1. What do you think was lacking in the conversation with Joni and Claris?

    a. *Why did the discussion get out of control?*

    b. *What could they have done better to avoid such a heated confrontation?*

2. Do you think Carlton's parents are interfering in his life? *Explain.*

3. Should Karen accept the cultural differences or find someone who has the same values?

    a. *What would you have done?*

4. Do you think young adults should leave home at the age of majority?

5. What are the problems with Cheryl and Pauline?

    a. *How can they be resolved?*

6. Describe one major method for conflict management.

6

Different Types of Conflict

Conflicts occur in various categories and forms depending on the *nature* of the event, the *place*, the *people* involved, and even the *timing*. Any of these conditions will make a difference to determine the decision whether to respond, the method to be used, and the emotional outcome after an assessment of the event. Below is a brief list of the different types of conflict.

Procrastination

This type of conflict relates to the timely receipt of correct data, facts, and other important requirements needed for solutions and other situations. Usually the cause for this conflict also includes unpunctuality, misunderstanding and misinformation. (For Example: *Student repeated lateness handing in papers; lack of interest, and so forth*).

Values Conflict

When this type of conflict occurs, it is often more difficult to resolve because it could be a violation of personal ethics and beliefs. People have to decide what they will accept and tolerate and what they will not. Keep in mind that although a mediator may help with a solution, there is no certainty that individuals will change their values. The outcome could be that each respects the other with the decision to recognize differences and certain acceptable behaviours.

(*It may also be that a student feels disrespected by the teacher or a peer after a harmless remark because he or she is from a different religious background*).

Interpersonal Conflicts

This occurs between individuals closely connected with each other at home, school, church, and work, and so on. Usually, this type of conflict centers on resources, social interactions, needs, values, jealousies, and personality differences. Individuals in those situations have expectations that they perceive will be in their best interest. (*Interpersonal conflict can sometimes be extremely selfish especially when one person has a need which he or she believes is being hindered by another*).

Social and Cultural

In this environment, you will find group cohesiveness, stereotyping, ostracization, and isolation. This could be the result of misunderstanding of cultural differences, educational levels, personal opinions; personal needs, lack of diversity skills, economic and language barriers.

(*We will not be able to avoid cultural conflicts since international travels have increased resulting in various cultural mix. These conflicts are created from language barriers, causing misunderstandings and difficulty interacting with those who are from different geographical regions. Some have inherent beliefs against certain people which may be difficult to hide or break. Therefore, conflict will occur if someone feels that he or she was treated unfairly*).

Intra-psychic

This is internal conflict, which causes frustration, dissonance, internal struggles, and confusion concerning personal values and making choices. This also includes situations such as personal need for belongingness, love, respect, and recognition. (*When people do not express themselves or find ways to resolve things which trouble them, they internalize those feelings. This can result in dissonance which will be reflected in their interaction with others*).

Intra-group Conflict

This type of conflict is among group members. When there is power struggle in a group, distrust, poor communication, and control. In this setting you will also find the situation of groupthink when members accept conflict to keep the peace, for the group to remain intact.

(*This type of conflict, if left unresolved, will create an atmosphere of instability. People will be on edge and there will be a lack of trust and confidence among them. It is this type of conflict which can result in division among group members with one set gravitating to a particular leader and the other set going in another direction*). (See I Corinthians 1: 11-13).

Discussion

1. Students could be asked to give a synopsis on each type of conflict from a realistic situation. They can use personal experience, a television program, or any other event which will bring out their understanding of each conflict.
2. Why is it important to know the type of conflict before attempting to resolve the situation?
3. Why should you obtain facts before trying to resolve a conflict?
4. What do you understand by dissonance, and how can this situation be resolved in an individual? What can that person do to bring harmony to his or her life?
5. How is interpersonal conflict different from intra-psychic conflict?
6. What are some of the dangers which might occur from intra-group conflict? How can this type of conflict be resolved?

Forgiveness is a
Conflict Resolution Method

And when ye stand praying, forgive, if ye have ought

against any: that your Father also which is in heaven

may forgive you your trespasses.

But if ye do not forgive, neither will your Father which

is in heaven forgive your trespasses.

Mark 11:25-26

7

Conflict Resolution Styles

The outcome of any conflict situation depends on the style used to respond to problems. This means that no one should attempt to resolve a conflict before finding out its nature, the substance, the people involved, and whether it can be resolved with the disputants or if there will be a need to have outside intervention.

Conflict of itself is harmless, but can become difficult and destructive if it is not handled in a proper manner and with the right methods. When there are problems with the resolving of a conflict, it could be that the individuals attempted to use a sledge hammer to kill an ant, which caused damage to an object.

Conflict does not have to be destructive when it occurs. Therefore, after acquiring all the facts about a dispute, deciding on the right method is essential for success in its resolution even when each person does not receive what he or she desired.

In the school setting, teachers of the conflict management program should teach students the various ways conflict will occur, and the methods which can be used to resolve those situations. If people are shown other ways for dealing with problems from those whom they respect and trust, there will be compliance and repetition as the technique for success is reinforced.

From the biblical perspectives, there are several methods given to resolve conflicts both in the <u>Old</u> (Proverbs; Exodus 20; Genesis 13:8); and <u>New Testaments</u> (Philippians 2:3; James 3:16; Matthew 5-7).

The Scriptures give Christian educators a wide array of examples and teaching principles relating to conflict management; whether interpersonal or otherwise to create methods and techniques for students' learning.

There are five basic styles for conflict resolution, often used alternatively, singly, or in combination depending on the situation and circumstance. Since not all conflicts are the same, the methods used for one situation may not work for another one, which may seem similar, but different in substance and nature.

Avoidance/*Non-confrontational*

This is when an individual does not wish to cause any problems. That person ignores issues and overlooks problems. The aim is to avoid confrontation at all costs. The person in this situation may also be trying to maintain a religious belief by displaying patience to avoid conflict. There is no indication that the conflict may go away.

Competitive/*Selfish*

In this style, the individual has no respect for the needs of others. The goal is to win regardless of who gets hurt. Every action is for a win/lose outcome with a confrontational aggressive demeanour. This is the type of situation that will evolve into conflict, and create a hostile environment for everyone.

Compromising/*Cooperative*

In this situation, the person is accepting, and cooperative despite the ongoing problems. The main interest is for the needs of others rather than personal. This individual will not threaten or attack. Instead, the aim is for a win/win outcome. Since not everyone is sincere, and honest. Therefore, someone may accept this behaviour for a while, but will eventually ignore it by showing disrespect for the person who is trying to keep the peace by compromising with hurtful situations.

Accommodating/*Non-assertive*

With this style, the individual is cooperative and non-assertive with willingness to give in even at the cost of personal desires or goals. There is compliance to demands in an effort to maintain calmness. Another reason for accommodating could be the natural personality of the individual. In such a case, there will most certainly be emotional abusive situations occurring. The reason is that an insensitive person may take the quiet and passive individual's personality for granted, and disrespect him or her. This can happen in school with peers, and in other settings where there are people working together.

Collaborating/*Problem solving*

With this style, the focus is on mutuality. Each one seeks the good of the other by combining ideas and resources. There is dialogue with options to maintain unity and respect for each other. [See Philippians 2: 3].

Discussion

Give examples of conflict resolution styles in each of the following situations.

1. Your best friend Joylene accidentally upsets a glass of water on the teacher's desk while she was seeing to another student. You are the only one who saw the incident, but kept quiet. The teacher was upset and blames the student. *How could you resolved this situation to avert further conflicts?*

2. You do not understand the new math problem; but do not want to bother the teacher, although she is not quite clear with her explanations. Everyone likes the teacher, so you prefer not to show up the mistakes made by her. *Is there a way you could seek help if you were scared of facing the teacher?*

3. Nancy is very bold and does not care about anyone else. From the back of the class she shouts out that she needs help with the new math problems. While the teacher is helping another student, she continues to disturb the class. Allan is quiet, and sees the problem that will arise if someone does not do something concerning Nancy. He went over and offered to help her. *Describe his action and style.*

4. When do you think each of those styles would be applicable?

8

The Characteristics of Conflict

One of the most important features about conflict is that it has values that can influence or change a relationship where there have been interpersonal discords. Its occurrence could be the main source for discovery of underlying misunderstandings, which may have been the cause for a dispute. It will also reveal how a destructive behaviour affects other people to result in drastic social changes in school, families, relationships, church, community, and anywhere groups gather for social activities.

Moreover, the exposure and successful management of problems will result in harmony and improved interpersonal relationships. Its positive effect in groups will empower members with challenges to be assertive in using skills to create unity, and mutual agreement for the best solutions when problems occur.

A conflict can disclose communication weaknesses in groups, between teachers and students, parents, and children, and among friends. It can also reveal needs which may have been suppressed by someone or others due to fear of disclosing those situations.

The cause of a conflict may help to reveal other problems and thereby help to maintain cohesiveness with emphasis on demonstration for respect, and trust for increased awareness of responsibility when group problems exist. It gives an intense desire to resolve issues without verbal insults or physical violence. The skillful handling of conflict will build and improve healthier cognitive, emotional, social, and psychological development.

Individuals will be better able to deal with stress, and cope with circumstances which might otherwise have been offensive.

Evidently, healthy conflict gives an individual increased motivation and energy to take a proactive approach when a problem arise. This action leads to a higher quality of interpersonal relationship, better group health, and community involvement.

Despite its destructive nature, conflict can bring about changes in any group setting and for personal development when it is managed constructively. This will lead to successful personal achievement, clear understanding, and defined goals.

9

Proactive and Reactive Conflict Responses

When a hurtful event occurs, the response will either be proactive or reactive. With being *proactive*, the individual adopts a calm and patient attitude towards the situation and does not act hastily. This does not suggest responding with passivity, nor will the individual ignore a problematic issue.

Instead, there is a desire to find an amicable resolution to restore peace and harmony. That person will critically assess the problem to arrive at the best solution for everyone. With such an attitude, the aim is for a win/win outcome with joint collaboration in an effort to find reasons and causes with the desire to change an uncomfortable situation.

Disputants will communicate feelings through collaborative discussions to help each one acknowledge both positive and negative behaviours. They do not attack each other with verbal assaults; but take time to listen and ask questions.

The objective is to create trust and confidence in the relationship. The proactive person shows respect for each person's opinion, with open discussion, effective listening, open-ended questioning, options, explanation, empathy, brainstorming, inclusion, involvement, and cooperation. If these are lacking, the outcome will be conflict, which might be destructive.

In contrast, with the *reactive* response, there is no thought, consideration, or concern for the feelings of others. That person acts impulsively, and does not care about the consequences. What and who are most important is to express feelings without care for anyone else, and the need for being right even when the individual is wrong.

The response is aggressive, and might even become physical preceded by the use of hurtful words. The main interest is about the self and the perception of the event, whether logical or otherwise. That individual acts irresponsibly according to emotions or the immediate interpretation of a disagreement.

The person may angrily express hurt and resentment causing the conflict to escalate. There is no thought or concern for timing or place for expression, who is present, or who will be hurt from a thoughtless action. In fact, actions are spontaneous, accompanied by insulting language used against an offender resulting in the breakdown of communication.

The thoughtless individual's behaviour will intensify the effect of a dispute that might have had a more favourable outcome after careful reflection and rational action.

Occasionally, the hurt individual seeks only for win/lose or lose/lose outcomes. In the first situation, the offended has the advantage. With the second method, no one wins to the desire of the reckless individual. In the second situation, there will be evidence of intimidation, emotional outbursts, anger, arguing, and other negative behaviours.

Marlene and Devon

Marlene and *Devon* are dating. They are both in their late teens with plans for college.

Although the relationship is reasonably upbeat, there are discrepancies on both sides.

Marlene wants *Devon* to go with her to the church picnic on Saturday, a few days away.

Despite Marlene's request, he had other plans to be with his friends from the basketball team.

Marlene thought he was ignoring her for shapely *Peony* who has been giving him smiles on the side.

Marlene is a little heavy set; but attractively shaped. However, instead of finding out the reason for the reluctance for not going with her, *Marlene* made a scene when she saw *Devon* talking with *Peony*.

She approached them with an onslaught of offensive threats and insulting words towards *Devon*.

Finally, she calmed down and *Peony* explained to her that she wanted information about *Devon's* friend *Charlie*.

Devon was very embarrassed, but remained cool.

Discussion

1. Identify *proactive* and *reactive* responses to conflict in the scene above.
2. What do you think was in Marlene's mind?
3. Do you think she cared about hurting Devon with her outburst?
4. Do you see win/win, win/lose/; lose/lose outcomes anywhere?
5. Describe Peony's response to Marlene.
6. Do you think what she did the right thing? How would you have responded to her?
7. Describe Devon's and Peony's attitude when Marlene approached them with her outburst of anger.

8. What could have been different concerning her approach?

9. What are some ways in which the situation could have been dealt with by Marlene?

10. What are some ways in which Devon and Peony could or might have responded to Marlene?

11. Think of the best solution for this incident.

10

Communication and Conflict

Interpersonal relationship is the association between two or more persons. The relationship does not have to be close especially if it is in a work or school setting, but there are social ethics for each individual to respect. Effective interpersonal relationship is vital to the social system, whether in the home or otherwise. We cannot live by ourselves without interacting with others.

This interaction is by way of communication either [*visually*] face-to-face; [*audibly*] telephone; [*media*] television, radio, or by letters, memos, pictures, and symbols [*written*].

We communicate even by our actions and behaviours, the way we treat one another, and many ways where others are involved. It is from these situations that conflicts often occur because of personal differences, misunderstandings, impulsiveness, and other factors.

Nevertheless, communication is necessary because we all have various needs such as physical, safety, social, practical, self-esteem, or self-actualization, which we can help to meet for one another.

We also communicate with each other for a sense of belonging, love, socialization, information, to achieve goals, aspirations, pleasure, relaxation, and entertainment. It is through the medium of communication that we interact and socialize so that we can function successfully in the home, public, and society.

Communication Styles

Although parents may love their children, some of them do not know how to communicate in a positive and loving way. There are parents with low self-esteem, which will affect the way they relate to the children. Since children go to school and socialize with others from varying backgrounds and cultures, they may not accept their parents' poor communication skills which they experience in the home.

In some situations, parents display their feelings of low self-esteem to their children. This will affect the flow and style of communication which will enhance positive interpersonal relations or negatively affect those interactions. The style of communication depends on people's perception of the world.

Therefore, the college student whose parents are not skilled in communication may be embarrassed to bring their colleagues home. Interpersonal communication is a vital factor in the home and society, and will affect everyone we encounter in whatever manner it is displayed.

Despite the different styles used in communication, some of those will prevent conflict; while others will create conflict which might be destructive. *This also refers to teachers to their students both in the school and college settings, and in the church community from leaders and members towards each other.*

Nevertheless, the different styles used may include the following:

1. *The Conciliator or Appeaser:* this person avoids conflict in order to be accepted by others. He or she seeks for every possible way to keep the peace, and will overlook wrongs. *This action will not prevent conflicts, and might even be the cause.*

2. *The Critic or Accuser:* this person will not accept responsibility, but finds faults about everyone else besides the self, and will openly accuse others without facts or reasons.

3. *Self-righteous communication:* this is someone who uses spirituality against others; especially those who do not attend church. This style will create interpersonal conflicts.

4. *Pretender:* this is a parent who claims to love all the children; but there is that *special* one who receives most of the attention. This causes emotional pain for the one who is ignored; whether it is in the home or school setting.

5. *Consistent communication:* this person is fair and trustworthy, whose confidence and genuine advice will be sought when conflicts occur.

6. *Confrontation:* this refers to consistent face-to-face communication, which builds strong interpersonal relationship.

7. *Triangulation:* using a go-between [*mediator, intermediary,* or *arbitrator*] to transfer information to another. In this situation, parents normally triangulate the weakest and most vulnerable of their children to carry out this behaviour. Usually mom and dad are not getting along, and a child will be used to relay information, one from the other.

Discussion

1. Describe the type of communication style used in your family?
   a. Do you believe this works for everyone?
   b. What would you change if it is not working?
2. How do you relate to your parents/ siblings?
   a. Are you satisfied with the style that you use?

    b. Do you think your parents or siblings communicate with you effectively?

3. How do you handle conflicts which occur in your relationships?

4. From the styles identified in this Chapter, select from drama or other scenes the communication style/s evident in the program.

5. What do you do when someone tries to use you as a mediator to facilitate his or her subjective attitude towards the other person? If this were your close friend or a relative, what would you do?

6. How would you deal with a situation where your friend suddenly cuts off all ties with you without explanation?

7. What do you do when there are conflicts in the home?

    a. Do you try to prevent being involved?

    b. Do you try to resolve the situation, or do you think it is none of your business?

    c. How do you think conflict in the home should be managed if you are not satisfied with the chosen style?

11

Non-violent Responses to Conflict

Interpersonal affiliation is one of the relationships where conflict will *always* occur because of differences in opinion, communication styles, needs, beliefs, values, and the close proximity of individuals. However, when there is a disagreement, there are ways in which this situation can be resolved without violence or verbal insults.

Unfortunately, this does not always happen because of personality differences and other factors. Even with longstanding friends and family members, there can be conflicts.

There are times when a slight error or misjudgment results in the breaking of a relationship which had great meaning to the people involved. We see this in marriages where spouses who were together for years suddenly break their long-standing commitment to each other, which may be due a slight misunderstanding where one person refuses to forgive.

Best friends fall out because one may not agree with the other, and decides it is time to quit. In any event, regardless of the situations, problems will occur at the best of times and at the worst of times. When those events happen, it will not be the substance which might cause the break in relationship, but the way in which the conflict was treated. This will either be in a *proactive* or *reactive* manner.

Resolving Interpersonal Problems

1. Before attempting to find a resolution for any dispute, you must first determine if there is a problem between you and the other person.

2. If you believe there is a problem, then set up a private face-to-face meeting for discussion. In some situations, you may need someone else to be present (Matthew 15).

3. Show respect and avoid shouting or embarrassing behaviours. Do not use hurtful words to describe the other individual. This will only escalate the conflict and cause more damage. The outcome itself may be costly more than you had anticipated if the relationship meant anything to you.

4. You can approach the situation in a non-insulting/threatening manner by calmly asking the other person if there is a problem.

    a. If the answer is "No." It is your turn to inform the person that you think there is a problem, and explain what you believe the problem to be. Show your reasons for concerns and why you called the meeting. The other individual may not notice that there are changes in his or her behaviour which affected you and your relationship with each other.
    b. As you talk with each other show regard, empathy, and listen for emotions: anger, sadness, sorrow and so forth. Pay attention and look each other in the eye without threats.

    c. If you are aware of a specific problem, which the other person has not admitted, do not "attack" with accusations. It would be better to calmly explain your side of the situation, and then wait for a response from the other individual.

5. Try to *listen* to each to other with open minds without pre-assessing the outcome or planning to attack. You might find that you maybe judging the individual, and will you not accept the explanation being offered.

    a. Be sure to *respect* each other's opinions without coercion or forcing yours on the individual.

    b. *Reflect* on the other person's opinion to find out if you have misjudged attitudes and behaviours.

    c. If the problem is one of misunderstanding or disrespect, try to determine why the other person felt disrespected by you. Explain any misunderstandings which may have caused the conflict to occur.

    d. Avoid blaming and pointing finger. Check your own attitude and behaviour, since no one is perfect, and we are unable to see our own faults (James 5:16).

6. Try to work out a compromise that pleases both of you so that the relationship can be mended.

How would you handle the following situations?

1. You saw Jack with a handful of books and offered to help. He responded abruptly with, "I don't need your help, I can manage alone."

2. Last week you told your sister about the new boy who came to your school. She told your mom who gave you a scolding about boys.

3. *Suzie* to *Tammy*, "What do you think of that hairdo, it is gorgeous?" speaking of *Jane* entering the room.

   Jane approached with a smile, but the other two girls burst out laughing because they saw *Collie* tripped and spilled a cup of coffee.

   Jane walked away feeling hurt.

12

Emotions

Emotions play a very significant function in conflicts both positively and negatively. They help us make decisions, and how to respond to situations which caused us discomfort or embarrassment. When applied appropriately, we are able to express our feelings about events without creating a conflict outcome. For example, we may respond with a frown, smile, laughter, anger, joy, happiness, share insults, embarrassments, and so forth. Some emotions are universal and unsociable, and we avoid expressing them openly.

There are many types of emotions which we experience, and some are communicable to others even without the spoken word; a smile or angry look sends a message to others. Despite their influence in a conflict event, emotions are natural situations in our lives which we experience every day.

Although there are times when we are hurt by circumstances, we can manage our emotions. One of the ways in which this is possible, is our awareness of what will make us angry, sad, or joyful.

Emotions will make us behave in ways which are comfortable, so that others understand us better. We too, have a responsibility to know how others feel, and the things that will excite or humiliate a friend or loved one.

Therefore, since we cannot read other peoples' minds, nor do we know everything about everyone, we learn social ethics for acceptable behaviours in order to maintain effective interpersonal relationships.

Some ways to manage Emotions in a given situation

1. *Feelings*: be truthful and acknowledge how you feel about a situation, but do not use hurtful offensive words.
2. *Empathy*: try to understand how the other person feels before making comments that will belittle and embarrass someone.
3. *Dignity*: maintain your self-respect, especially if you believe you are the better person.
4. *Be specific*: do not over-generalize. Express yourself so that the other person understands what you are saying. Avoid innuendoes and slurs.
5. *Honesty*: be truthful when relating your part in a dispute.
6. *Responsibility*: Do not blame someone else if you are at fault. Accept your faults with honesty so that others can trust you.
7. *Self-control*: do not act impulsively. It will cause a breakdown in a relationship, or you may hurt someone in anger.
8. *Sensitivity*: treat others the way you would want them to treat you.

13

The Role of Emotions in Conflict

We often communicate through our emotions which express the way we feel about an encounter or someone who might be pleasant or unpleasant to us. This makes emotions to be the instigator for any type of conflict to occur, especially when they become out of control. When we do not control our emotions we create strife, malice, murmuring, complaining, and become unthankful, with display of mean dispositions of unkindness, and unpleasantness. If those situations are left to mature into significant events to affect other people, conflict will be the outcome. This will happen in relationships, school, the workplace and at home.

Additionally, our character is expressed in our emotions and behaviour. The way we communicate with others can be a source of effective problem solving, or a hindrance. The role of emotions then can be considered as expressive contributors to conflict situations: either to calm hurts, or to cause destructive behaviours. Nevertheless, we do not have to allow our emotions to get out of control. Instead, we can learn to manage the way we feel about insults, and express ourselves about other peoples' treatment toward us with dignity.

Primarily, the decision rests with us to respond in a manner that will not be destructive, but effective for others to understand our concerns about injustices. While there may be justifiable reasons to express objections to unfairness, this does not mean we should make other people feel uncomfortable with unsociable behaviours.

Some conflicts are the result of assumptions and ineffective communication patterns. They include non-verbal communication such as raised eyebrows, silence, and a clenched fist. Even a smile at the wrong time may cause someone to be angry. These all communicate the way people feel about something which is offensive to them; and may be the cause for a conflict situation.

Nevertheless, while someone may be offended, there is always a time and place to express feelings and hurts. We express displeasure with non-verbal behaviours, or respond with angry emotional outbursts, making those around us uncomfortable or even fearful.

Occasionally, we even blame ourselves for allowing indignities to us, and this will make us angry. This type of anger if internalized, will lead to intra-psychic conflict which will eventually hurt us or cause us to explode at the wrong time to the wrong person. It is from those internalize feelings which can result in dissonance causing frustration and anger.

Patricia sat at the dining room table preparing for a test. In walked her brother *Eric* with his iPod blaring. He really did not notice that *Patricia,* who had her back to him, was preparing for a test. He tapped her on the shoulder in salutation, but she did not look up. Instead, she acknowledged him with "hi" and went back to her work. This was not good enough for *Eric* who took an offence to her behaviour thinking his sister was brushing him off. He confronted her and pulled the book in front of her from off the table.

It made *Patricia* "mad." She struck at *Eric*, who ducked, and the book fell out of his hand losing its cover and a few pages. She was fuming, as she looked at Eric who was taller and of course stronger. She made an attempt to attack, but held back.

Although *Patricia* was upset, she contained her anger, retrieved the book, and continued with her studies. *Eric* was extremely sorry and apologized to his sister. *Patricia* looked at her brother, and nodded that she accepted his apology. Eric left feeling very sorry; and crest-fallen.

Discussion

Why was Patricia upset with Eric since he did not ruin the book out of spite? Do you think it would have been justifiable to attack Eric? Why, why not? Identify the emotions displayed in the scene, and the role they played in Patricia's decision? Do you think that Eric's apology was sufficient?

14

Anger and Conflict

Anger is an emotion which plays a substantial role in the escalation of a conflict, and the major factor for a destructive outcome from a disagreement. The reason is that anger contains blind fury, wrath, intense rage, and unreasonable haste. It is the result of passion with the desire to set matters straight, to seek vindication, and or to get even quickly.

The angry person will sometimes be cruel with the use of harsh words, and might incite others to physical fight with teasing and jeering to make the other person angry. Nevertheless, despite its function in conflict situations, anger is a controllable emotion if the individual is aware of cues and signals that will influence its emergence.

Moreover, nothing is wrong about being angry; but the emotion must be constrained; otherwise it can become destructive. Ephesians 4:26, "(Be ye angry), and (sin not): *let not the sun go down on your wrath.*"

The destructive side of anger acts like a vicious beast, which can be deadly, fierce, cruel, volatile, violent, and even provocative. When anger becomes destructive, it behaves similar to a volcano, spreading lava all around. It burns, and injures those in its path.

An angry person does not think about actions or the consequences following an inconsiderate behaviour. The main interest of the angry person is the desire for immediate response to insults or other situations. Anger brings about results that can be severe and deadly.

The outcomes from an angry event may be injuries and even loss of lives. Socially, there are broken relationships, separation of siblings, parents and children, divorce, and various other situations; all due to a moment of impulsive uncontrolled anger.

Anger is costly in many ways; financially, socially, mentally, and spiritually. Therefore, think twice before giving way to passions that will embarrass or cause injury.

Features of Anger

Since anger plays such a critical role in conflict situations, everyone should pay attention if there is evidence of its imminent occurrence. Otherwise, it might become destructive and uncontrollable. When anger gets out of control, people say the wrong things, tempers become elevated, and it may cause physical encounters. The description of anger has three main features *expressed*, *suppressed*, or *unexpressed*.

Expressed Anger

Expressed anger often occurs through various forms of body language such as raised eyebrows, a clenched fist, shoving, hitting, the tone of voice, and the chosen words.

Furthermore, there are times when this expressive behaviour becomes volatile and destructive; but it is possible to control it no matter what the circumstances were that caused the emotion. In order for the individual to be calm, that person must control negative thoughts and the feelings which accompany them. Paul gave a simple, yet powerful principle in Philippians 4:8.

Finally, brethren, whatsoever things (are) true, whatsoever things (are) honest, whatsoever things (are) just, whatsoever things (are) pure, whatsoever things (are) lovely, whatsoever things (are) of good report; if (there be) any virtue, and if (there be) any praise, think on these things.

There are times when just pausing to think before a response will ease tension, and cause the anger to dissipate. This will lessen hurt feelings and *physiological* arousal caused by the anger. Some of those arousals will make the individual perspire profusely; there is tightness in the chest, changes in the body, stomach ache, rapid pulse, raised blood pressure, facial expression, tightening of the muscles, posture, and so on, aroused by anger.

Suppressed Anger

This is covert because the individual internalizes hurt feelings even with a smile. Unknown to others, the person may be fuming on the inside and planning a way for retaliation. This type of anger is dangerous, and often erupts without warning. It can also be an indication of passive aggression when the individual pretends and does not express feelings until one day there is an eruption with no warning. Suppressed anger can lead to dissonance and various other destructive situations.

Unexpressed

Unexpressed anger can create other problems. These could include expressions, such as *passive-aggressive behaviours* by planning to attack or exhibiting behaviours that are sarcastic, distrustful, suspicious, and hostile. People who are constantly putting others down, criticizing everything, and making disparaging comments have not learned how to express their anger constructively.

Discussion

1. Describe the emotion of anger.
2. Is anger a bad thing? Explain your answer.
3. Be creative and give advice concerning the best way to manage a hurtful event without causing embarrassment to the self or others.

Students can describe situations which make them angry. Ask them how they manage anger when it happens.

4. What are some destructive ways for managing anger?
5. What are some constructive anger management techniques?
6. What are the situations that will cause anger?
7. How does anger erupt in a relationship?
8. What do you do when you are angry?
9. What do you do when others are angry at you?

15

Some Reasons for Anger

There are many reasons why someone will become angry. These include insecurity, uncertainty about the future, feelings of disrespect, losses, resentment, jealousy, envy, pride, disappointment, and past hurts. Including are times when anger is triggered from the way an individual assesses an unfair event. Nevertheless, despite what happens in life, each person must take charge of the emotion of anger to avoid injuring others with impulsive outbursts.

Reasons for Anger

Blaming Others

There are times when an individual will be angry with the world, and for this reason, he or she will be angry with anyone who crosses the path.

    a.   It is better to look within oneself to find out what part you played to cause the angry outburst of the other person.

    b.   Do not blame others when you have made mistakes.

    c.   Another way in which we blame others occurs when we do not manage time properly and we are late for an event. While individuals may contribute to our problems, we have control over our own emotions, affairs, and life and should act responsibly as much as we are able.

    d.   Change any negative thoughts about people, God, the world, and yourself.

Poor Attitude

Some people believe that everyone owes them something. They make unfair demands on others, and when those persons fail them, they become angry because of the disappointment.

> *Dale left school at age 15 and never went back. He is in a low-paying job with no hopes of promotion because he does not have the qualifications. Although he has been encouraged to return to school, he has always rejected the idea. He complains that no one cares about him, and everyone is against him. He is moody and is a constant worry to the family.*

Personal Difficulties

Everyone faces difficulties and situations which seem insurmountable at times. Some people are able to cope and maybe make changes to ease some of the pressures they face. However, there are others who do not face problems with commonsense and diplomacy. Instead, they expect everyone to respond to their needs. When this does not happen, they project their anger towards life or someone else gets the blame.

  a. Seek out people who can help you with your problem.
  b. Ask for assistance: parent, older sibling, teacher, friend, pastor, or any person who is willing to advise and guide you into the right path. You could also do research on the internet to find answers, especially when seeking scholarships.
  c. Do not doubt your abilities. You will not know what you can do until you try.

Ineffective Communication

Frequently, misunderstandings and miscommunication will create the atmosphere for anger. Effective communication will establish an environment for discussions and asking questions. However, if people do not respect one another and there is shouting and anger, nothing will be achieved, causing hostilities and animosities to prevail.

When an angry person becomes loud and emotional, it is better to remain calm rather than add fuel to the situation.

    a.   Think carefully before speaking to avoid the temptation of being rash as this will escalate conflict and make matters worse.

    b.   Choose your words with much thought before speaking. Be empathetic, and patient.

    c.   Listen for emotions in a conversation, and reflect before responding to understand what might have caused the angry outburst.

    d.   Ask pertinent questions before jumping to conclusions. One moment of patience can save a life-time relationship.

    e.   As much as you are able, remain calm; but be precise while being thoughtful and gentle without sarcasms or to convey any condescending tones.

Feeling of Self-Importance

Angry people tend to believe that the world spins around them. They do not listen to the opinions of others, because they consider themselves always right, even when they are blatantly wrong. Here again, patience is required to relate the right message with the hope that the individual will understand.

    a.   Never think yourself to be better than anyone else because of the expertise or gifts which you have.

    b.   Do not compare yourself with those who cannot measure up to your abilities, opportunities, or position in life.

    c.   Learn to be humble. You will win lasting friends as opposed to when you feel yourself better than others.

Environmental Causes

The immediate surroundings may be the cause for frustration and rage. Problems and responsibilities can weigh heavily to trigger cues for angry outbursts. Each person should be aware of emotional warnings before becoming inflamed with anger.

    a. Although there are times when governmental, family, or other situations arise which you cannot change. Do not allow them to impede you.

    b. There is always a way out of even poverty if you apply yourself to aspire to be successful.

    c. Even though situations may interrupt your life; do not allow them to be the end of your hopes. Keep trying until you succeed, even if it takes a while to arrive to where you want to go.

Stressful Situations

Anger can be the result of anxiety and emotional strain caused by stress. There is nervous tension, agitation, frustration, and constant worry if there are unmet needs. Similar to anger, stress is normal, but there are reasons that will cause it to occur.

    a. The way to manage stress is to plan, and set priorities.

    b. Get up on time to do chores or for school.

    c. What are the situations that bring on stress?

    d. Identify the stressors and learn self-control.

Describe Dale's *disposition and explain why you believe he behaves the way he does. How would you advise him about anger?*

16

Anger Management

"Be not hasty in thy spirit to be angry: for anger rests in the bosom of fools" (Ecclesiastes 7:9).

Anger is an emotion, which often becomes destructive. The reason is that many people do not know how to manage this emotion, and therefore it gets out of hand. In some situations, the angry person will disturb others with unsociable behaviours causing shame, embarrassment, and harm. People often act in haste when they are offended. They are impetuous and are always making amends for thoughtless words and careless actions. An impulsive word or act can result in a life-time of misery.

Nevertheless, to be angry is not a sinful act, unless the individual cause physical hurt or verbally insults others with biting words. It is always best to wait, think, weigh a matter, consider the consequences and outcome before making sudden judgments, or making important decisions.

When anyone senses the emergence of anger, it is better to take a walk or do something constructive to avert destructive behaviours and prevent unnecessary hurt feelings. Most importantly, you do not have to use insulting words or foul language to express your objection to someone or something, which disturbs your peace of mind.

Ideas for Managing Anger

- *Pause before* Responding: When you delay to respond to anger, it is the easiest way to deal with the emotion.

- *Timing*: Choose a suitable time for dealing with delicate situations.

- Avoidance: Some situations are not worth your time, leave them alone, and move on. You do not have to respond to everything which is said. There are times when a response is not necessary. Silence can be more effective!

- *Leave the Past* Behind: Rid yourself of bad memories, and do not allow them to take up residence in your thoughts.

- *Forgive*: Forgive the aggressor and pray that he or she learns to deal with anger.

- *Owning* Up: Admit to your part in the dispute. Do not hide your feelings or bottle them up.

- *Express your* Feelings: Vent constructively in a safe place by doing something physical such as mopping, cleaning the garage, etc. Do not hurt others or destroy property.

- *Thought Management*: Change the way you think about people and events (Philippians 4:8). Angry people tend to curse, swear, or speak with terms that reflect their inner thoughts. Do not try to change people; but you can change your negative thoughts and your behaviour.

- *Control Emotions*: Acknowledge and deal with your feelings in a responsible and sensible manner. Learn to control your reactions to a given situation.

17

Conflict Management

Since there are so many reasons which will cause conflict, when there is a dispute it is very important to identify the problem, and to focus on the issues, and not on the offender. It is also impossible to devise a structure for management to reach an acceptable resolution unless the source and context in which the conflict occurs are determined. Therefore, the issues must be carefully examined before making a decision concerning its management and resolution.

It is also important to find out the correct strategy to use according to the nature of the conflict. The reason is that all conflicts are not the same; nor can the same method be used for every situation. For example, the conflict could be interpersonal, personal interests, needs, values, opinions, physical problems, cultural, and so on.

Which means the most applicable approach for the type of conflict must be applied to reach an amicable outcome which is contingent upon the nature of the problem. This also includes the needs of the disputants and whether they will each accept the outcome after discussions.

Another very significant feature about conflict management is that although there are specific techniques, there is no one universal strategy to use for each circumstance because issues, people, and needs differ. Despite how the mediator may try, not everyone may be satisfied with the outcome; but the aim is to bring some closure to the argument.

Consequently, the disputants including mediator must pay close attention to manner, behaviour, and the words used in a discussion. Similar to the way conflict management styles differ, so is the management of a dispute.

Discuss the following:

You made a comment that you are "fed up, and will not put up with anymore of this nonsense." You were really referring to the mess in the room.

Susan entered the door and without asking what you are talking about and told Everton, who is the group leader, that you are very angry, and you are leaving the group. He saw you with your bag [you were going to the kitchen for a drink], he said, "Shut the door behind you when you leave."

1. What are some of the things happening in this scene?
2. Name the dynamics in the situation which will create anger, conflicts, contention, disrespect, misunderstanding, and so on.
3. Whether as the group leader, Susan or the one who made the comment, how would you handle this situation, to bring about an amicable resolution?

Managing a Conflict Situation

You may use an Objective Person such as a Mediator

1. Set ground rules for each person to follow;
2. Pay careful attention to the discussion;
3. Use open-ended questions for explanations, and not closed with "yes and no" answers;

4. Allow the other person to speak, but do not criticize;

5. Pay attention to body language, emotions, and attitudes;

6. Probe gently to find out if anyone is being positional; or if there are underlying needs;

7. Find out what usually provokes anger in your group;

8. Be respectful, and do not cast blame or use insults;

9. Listen with your emotions and senses;

10. Concentrate on the issues, reflect and be present;

11. Adjust your posture, and pay close attention to body language;

12. Be congruent with your responses;

13. Go beyond just hearing words.

14. Be reflective and sensitive to the feelings of others;

15. Each person must analyze individual behaviour;

16. Be flexible and open-minded;

17. If the responses to the conflict are not working, devise ways to change offensive behaviour;

18. Discuss various ways for meeting needs;

19. Devise options for solving the problem;

20. Brainstorm for options so that each person participates;

21. Make sure everyone understands the dispute;

22. Explain any agreement for a resolution so that everyone understands and is satisfied at the end;

23. Seek for win/win outcome;

24. Not every conflict situation will be resolved the way the disputants expected, or you the facilitator expected.

25. Always close with harmony, even if everyone did not receive what he or she wanted.

18

Conflict Management Skills

We will always have something in our lives which make us angry, uncomfortable, anxious and in various other emotional ways. While we all need comfort and peace in our lives, this is not always possible. People have needs, and there are those who will make their position known, which might affect other people in negative ways. When this happens, it might result in conflicts.

Conflicts are not really the cause of disputes; but the outcome from disagreements, and the manner in which those events are managed. Being able to resolve a situation positively is one of the best social skills an individual can display in the time of heated disputes.

Regardless of what the dispute is about, it does not have to be destructive if it is managed effectively with the use of the right methods. With the constructive management of conflicts, there are three specific skills, which include *negotiation, mediation, and arbitration.*

Negotiation

With this style, disputants meet to discuss their differences. The aim is to reach an amicable resolution for each party in the dispute. Each one must have a plan concerning needs and what he or she will accept, or reject.

For example:

James is *Maria's* brother. They are both teenagers 15 & 17 respectively, with taste for different genre of music.

James does not care for the religious kind his sister listens to, but prefers rap.

What upsets him most is that *Maria's* iPod is always at the highest level, which makes him very angry. He has complained to her several times, but the cessation is only temporary.

James decided to appeal to their parents. They too, are tired of the loud music early mornings, late at nights, and so on.

The family met in the den one evening to decide how they could come to an agreement to make things better for everyone.
Obviously, *Maria* wants to continue listening to her kind of music and so does James his.

The parents also want peace of mind. After a very heated discussion, the agreement reached was that *Maria* would listen to her music when she is outside of her room with the use of earphones. *James* will continue to enjoy rap.

The parents were happy for the peace and quiet; so everyone accepted this arrangement with each receiving what he or she wanted.

Settling disputes is not always an easy task, and some might be very violent and boisterous. However, the main focus must be for mutual agreement or at least, acceptance of an outcome.

Mediation

Mediation is an alternative method for intervention to reach an agreement in a dispute. Usually the aim is to get the disputants to communicate, which is the first breakdown in a relationship, whether at home, the workplace, school, or church. The disputants engage the services of a *mediator* who will listen <u>attentively</u> and <u>objectively</u> to the parties as they each communicate their differences in a non-threatening environment. This includes effective listening, questioning, respect, reflecting, and empathy.

The mediator <u>does not</u> solve the problem; but <u>facilitates</u> the discussion without passing judgment on any of the parties. At the end of the session, the mediator prepares an agreement that each disputant in the dispute must reads and understands before signing.

With *Maria* and *James* above, if the problem had become unresolved, they could have called another person to mediate the dispute.

Arbitration

Arbitration is really a last resort that may leave at least one person resentful and angry toward the arbitrator. Both parties must agree to this type of approach.

Discussion

1. Ask the students to describe each method listed above for the resolution of a dispute.
2. You could set up scenarios to depict each technique.
3. Devise illustrations with the use of each method. You can use role-plays which can be very effective when applied successfully.

If you profess to be a Christian,

follow the advice below:

But be ye doers of the word, and not hearers only,

deceiving your own selves.

James 1: 22

19

Communicating to De-escalate Conflict

Communication is the normal way in which we interact and relate to one another. For this action to be effective there must be a sender and receiver. However, since each person differs from the other with a wide range of personalities and needs, the meaning of a message maybe misinterpreted according to how the individual understands it. What causes conflict in communication is the way we respond to the misunderstanding of a message we receive. If we do not understand the content or the language used, this can result in problems.

Moreover, people identify us by our habits, and the way we communicate feelings and dissatisfaction. Still, to adopt an attitude of passivity when being hurt will not communicate the right feelings, nor would expressing our objections in anger help a heated situation, which will only make matters worse.

Admittedly, communication plays a vital role in conflict; and to avoid problems there must be a right way for expressing offenses without causing further distress. We know that by gently saying no, this attitude will ease a tensed situation, rather than being aggressive with words or negative body language.

When communicating, you may find that one person tries to impress another with innuendoes, pretense, and behaviours that can be insulting. It is better to be respectful, honest, truthful, sincere, and kind; instead of trying to convince someone in an attempt to outdo another person. It is also important to note that we need one another; and for this reason we should show respect, patience, and understanding.

If we recognize our own insufficiencies, we will do everything in our power to make life easier for others and ourselves. It is when we do not care about another person that we use unkind words to emotionally hurt, and at times physically attack the individual.

When conflicts arise, they can be from longstanding disagreements and issues which were left unresolved. Whatever the reasons for not dealing with those problems might be, the situations can result in conflicts which are often costly in a number of ways.

These include, financial, time, and the effect the conflict may have on a relationship in the family, school, church, or work. Every unkind word does not have to end in heated retorts. If we think before speaking, acting, or exploding, many situations which got out of hand would not have happened.

"*A soft answer turns away wrath: but grievous words stir up anger.*" (Proverbs 15:1).

"*Wherefore, my beloved brethren, let every man be swift to hear, slow to speak, slow to wrath:*" (James 1:19).

Steps for de-escalating Conflict

1. *Sensitivity:* effective communication to de-escalate conflict means you do not only try to get your thoughts expressed without care or for the interests and feelings of others; instead, you make every effort to understand the other person through feelings and sensitivity.

   a. Avoid being harsh and insensitive to the feelings of the other person in the dispute with you.

   b. Avoid making loose judgments about things which you have no knowledge about. Avoid biases and negatives.

   c. Always make eye contact because this shows respect.

   d. Be a person of truthfulness, integrity, trustworthiness, and reliability.

2. *Place:* choose a place for private discussion and make sure you know what you plan to say.

3. *Body language:* pay careful attention to your posture, and do not fold your arms or purse your lips. These are signs of arrogance, disrespect, and hostility.

4. By your body language, those present will know whether you are paying attention, or if you respect the other person.

5. *Tone:* speak softly, and do not shout or use bad language.

6. *Active Listening:* this does not mean that you must or will accept everything someone says; but it gives everyone the impression that you are present, by the questions you ask.

7. *Congruence:* state what you mean clearly without innuendoes or ambiguities. This will help to achieve a win/win outcome, which should be your aim.

8. There must be congruence with verbal and body language.

9. *Clarity:* ask questions for clarification and explanation, and allow others to do the same.

10. Remember that assumptions will not gain a win/win outcome since some may not understand everything.

11. *Paraphrase:* in some situations, you may have to paraphrase in order to clarify statements from the other person in the dispute. Use "I" statements, rather than "you said…."

    For example, "*Sally,* did I hear you say that people are insensitive to your feelings?"

    <u>Rather than</u>, "You said no one cared about you!"

12. *Language/Words/Slangs:* avoid using words and technical jargons which everyone does not understand. Always pay attention to religious, cultural, age, and other differences which might have caused the conflict in the first place. Be sensitive to these features since ignoring them may create greater problematic situations. Therefore, choose your words for *clarity* and *understanding* for everyone.

20

Four Step Conflict Resolution

A. Confrontation

1. Decide how you will approach the issue.
2. Select a place away from others nearby to avoid eavesdroppers.
3. There must be mutual agreement on the process for resolution.
4. At the beginning of discussion, find out the cause for the conflict.
5. Pay careful attention to your behaviour with effective listening.
6. Be flexible without being harsh, judgmental, name-calling or blame. Devise options for dealing with issues.
7. Be respectful and empathetic towards the other party.
8. Be sensitive to feelings and discomfort.

B. Questioning

1. Design your questions to avoid ambiguity or intimidation.
2. Probe gently with open-ended questions of when, what, and how, to describe what happened, and how the person felt.
3. Avoid closed questions with "yes" and "no" responses.
4. Make sure that everyone understands each question.
5. Leave room for clarification and explanation.
6. Be honest when describing your own feelings.

C. Effective Listening

1. Allow the other party to finish speaking.
2. Do not interrupt or interject. Keep an open mind - be selective, reflective, patient, and respectful.
3. Ask for explanations, and give feedback when appropriate.
4. Be receptive to other communication styles, summarize, clarify, reframe.

5. Be fair, and give the same amount of time to each person.
6. Do not take sides or impose your own beliefs and values.
7. Be specific with answers to questions, and do not generalize.
8. Pay attention to your body language. Be congruent.

D. Resolution Process

(i). Examine your *Perception* of the Issues. *Was the conflict*:

Inevitable, Avoidable; Destructive; or Manageable

(ii.) Examine the *Events* with the disputants. *Check for*

1. Timing of events
2. Possible causes and or prevention

(iii). Orderliness – *Set Ground Rules*

1. Allow each person to speak.
2. Avoid being impatient.
3. Explain your position

(iv). Brainstorm to reach an amicable *resolution*

1. Ask questions
2. Evaluate the options

(v). Resolution

a. Ask what each person needs, decide how they will be met, and what each person will do.
b. Ensure that everyone understands what he/she has to do to restore the relationship.
c. Set clear, specific, and reachable goals.
d. Present your expectations.
e. Obtain feedback and commitment from each one.
f. Ask for a written commitment if possible.

21

Assertiveness and Conflict Management

Assertiveness is a non-destructive technique used for effectively managing a conflict. The assertive person is not hostile, but seeks for win/win outcomes. It means that words are carefully chosen to avoid causing friction, but with sincerity and preciseness. The individual is able to *affirm clear intentions* concerning something that might be wrong. For example, if your friend *Jackie* encourages you to take drugs, which are destructive, you will confidently say "no" without being aggressive.

In another situation, a friend may want you to do something that is immoral. Instead of cursing the person and using words to demean or condemn, you will take your friend aside and show him the dangers of participating in such behaviour. In the end, you might win your friend's respect, rather than gain an enemy by being aggressive. A major attribute to the assertive person is the *ability to influence* others in terms of using authority in a positive manner to guide, teach, and control. This is where the individual uses leadership skills to motivate and help another person.

The assertive person will not use manipulative methods to benefit selfish purposes with no regard for the welfare of others. That person allows principles and standards of behaviours relating to interpersonal relationships to direct him or her. There is evidence of leadership values that will influence and encourage others to do the right thing.

These includes factors of sincerity, loyalty, and honesty, displayed effectively even if a best friend wants the individual to detour from what is moral and upright living. Besides, the assertive person will avert conflicts by displaying integrity in his interactions. He admits to faults and is not afraid to apologize for personal mistakes.

Evidently, he recognizes how crucial integrity is required for building character, and alleviating conflict. Integrity means honesty, truthfulness, and reliability. With these, we can include punctuality. Many people do not understand that unpunctuality is disrespect of other people's time. It is a signal to those who expect you to arrive on time that you do not care about them, and they must accept your behaviour or leave you alone. This type of attitude will create the atmosphere for conflicts.

Therefore, the assertive person will be conscious of not causing distress and disharmony, and will consider the feelings of those quiet non-assertive persons. They do not violate or take advantage because of their weakness to represent themselves in a given situation.

Assertiveness teaches effective communication without causing offense. If someone made a statement such as, "*I am not happy with this decision, could we change it?*" as opposed to, "*I do not want this, and you had better change it,*" there is a difference with the tone in each statement. The first statement displays respect and thoughtfulness for the other person's feelings, while the second expresses aggressiveness and lack of concern for the other individual.

Another point about being assertive is that it is a non-violent, non-aggressive way for the reduction of conflict. Using this approach improves interpersonal relationship and strengthens friendships.

Furthermore, the assertive person is an independent thinker who maintains personal beliefs, opinion, and values no matter what others say. No one influences that individual, not even a parent who may want him or her to do something unethical. The assertive person is confident without being bossy or proud, with a measure of self-assurance that he is not breaking a law, or treading on another person's privacy. This is a person with high self-esteem who knows how to control emotions.

Although there will be times when the emotion of anger will emerge, he or she is in control with the ability to express opinions and views with respect, confidence, and courage without imposing his or her ideas on others. That person is confident of what he or she wants, and is not afraid to state those demands with politeness, decorum, and honesty when challenged.

Other Conflict Management Methods include the following:

Non-Assertiveness

The non-assertive person is fearful, timid, shy, and easily manipulated by others. The individual is not an independent thinker. Instead, he or she is passive towards others' treatment, and avoids confrontation. Although that person knows that abuse is wrong and is frustrated, yet there is no attempt to correct the situation. This is the type of person who will accept self-blame, and entertain anxiety that will cause stress because of emotional impediment to do anything about personal hurts and abuses.

Aggression

Some people respond to conflict with aggression. To be aggressive means making selfish demands or coercing others to do what you want them to do. The aggressive person is a controller who expresses thoughts, feelings, and beliefs without concern for the rights and feelings of others.

The behaviour is an expression of insecurity where the person wants to be first in everything. It does not matter who gets hurt, he must have what he wants, which is all that matters.

That person always seeks for the win-lose outcome where he has the advantage.

Including with this behaviour is the attitude for competitiveness because the emphasis is only on the individual, and not the needs or feelings of others. It is really a selfish way for dealing with conflict situations.

Discussion

In the scenes below, identify assertive, non-assertive, and aggressive behaviours.

Brenda is a loving and popular girl in school. She is smart, confident and has many friends. *Frank* asked her out on a date, but bluntly told her, "I will not go out with you and that horrible hairstyle." To be honest it was terrible, and did not suit her face.

Erick heard the conversation, and went over to her and said, "You are a beautiful girl with very nice hair. Would you like to go out with me on Saturday?"

Brenda was surprised because she was embarrassed about *Frank's* remark.

She turned to *Erick* and asked, "Do you like my hair like this?" He responded with, "If you like it and feel comfortable with it, then let no one change you." "However, if you want my honest opinion, why not ask your hair dresser to fix it a little differently so that it shows your beauty."

Three days later Frank saw Brenda, and said to her, "So I see that you took my advice…"

Suzie remarked, "*Brenda*, your hair looks beautiful…go girl!"

22

Assertive and Aggressive Exercises

Being assertive means the individual acts without coercion, but with confidence and self-esteem. The assertive person is clear, and precise, but not demanding. He or she is able to express thoughts and feelings without being aggressive, despite the outcome. There is concern for the rights and feelings of others with regard for weaknesses.

1. If you do not like the way someone treats you, express yourself, and do not beat around the issue. This behaviour shows insecurity, and in some cases, dishonesty. Instead of chuckling with someone who disrespects you, calmly

   a. Say "*Jolie, Stop.*"
   b. Say, "*Tubal, do not touch me again.*"

2. Avoid being indefinite or confusing. Rather, be extremely clear with your opinions and views so that there is no room for misunderstanding or ambiguity. State exactly what you mean that you do not want to drink alcohol, take drugs, watch pornography, or engage in any form of illicit sexual behaviours. Be firm with your rejection:

   Instead of saying,

   a. "I might, let me think about it." Say,

   b. *"I don't want to do it. Leave alone and do not ask me again."*

3. Do not hold on to a relationship if it is destructive to your values and beliefs. You do not have to buy a friend or lower your standards to gain a friend.

4. If you are with your "friends" and one of them is leading you astray, do not accuse the group for violating your space. Instead, direct your statement to the one who is encouraging you to do wrong. You must acknowledge who you are, and what you want. Be direct and honest with your confrontation with respect, noting the value and quality of the relationship.

    "Jack, I said that I do not smoke. Do not force me to do something I am against."

5. When stating your beliefs, values, and standards, express exactness, clarity, and honesty despite how others may think about you. Do not use words that are insulting and harsh.

6. If in your presence, someone says

    "I don't like people who are from … because I believe they are…." or *"I think Christians [?] are…"*

    If you do not agree, calmly state your own views.

    "I cannot agree with you concerning this matter and do not wish to continue with this conversation."

7. Even if this person is your friend, you do not have to smother your feelings or hide your beliefs to accommodate him or her.

8. Do not participate in the painful intolerant behaviours of prejudices or narrow-mindedness. It is hurtful to those who experience this conduct. *Do unto others, as you would have them do unto you.*

Assertiveness vs. Aggressiveness

Frequently when a dispute occurs in a relationship, it is normally from the thoughtless words, and angry behaviours exhibited from one person towards another. The offended person will become angry because there are feelings of violation and disrespect. However, if there were consideration for the feelings of others before speaking or acting, many relationships would survive. Another point is that some people often embellish and overstate incidents and events, this is wrong. State the facts, and do not improve to make yourself look good. Always maintain honesty and truthfulness.

Examples of assertive, and aggressive statements.

1. *"I wish you had not done it this way"* [Assertiveness]
   "Why did you do it this way? Don't you know better?" [Aggressive]

2. *"Judy, may I use your phone? Mine does not have internet"* [Assertiveness].
   "Judy, give me your phone so that I can use the internet. Mine does not have it" [Aggressiveness].

3. *"Mom, thanks for being so kind and thoughtful"* [Assertiveness]
   "Mom, you never remember my birthday" [Aggressiveness]

4. *"I see you are admiring my dress. Do you like it?"* [Assertiveness]
   "What are you looking at. [Aggressiveness]

5. *"I would like to make a statement"* [Assertiveness]
   "Shut up when someone is talking?" [Aggressiveness]

6. *"I am sorry for upsetting you. I did not mean to do it"* [Assertiveness and owning up]

"*You are making me lose my temper*" [<u>Aggressiveness</u> and not owning up to faults]. <u>No one</u> makes you lose your temper. <u>You, make the choice</u> to respond to aggression the way which suits you best.

7. "I don't understand what you are saying."

   "*Why don't you learn to express yourself so that others can better understand you?*"

8. "When you have time could you please explain this to me?"

   "*Hey Sue, I want you to explain this to me now?*"

9. "Would you help me with this?"

   "*Why are you so selfish? Can't you see that I need help?*"

10. "I did not like what you said this morning."

   "*Don't you ever speak to me like that again? I heard you this morning.*"

11. "I do not think it will work. It might be better doing it this way...

   "*Don't you know of a better way to do this thing? I can do it better.*"

23

Practice Forgiving Others

Forgiveness is one of the most effective methods for de-escalating conflicts. It will prevent the internal build-up of animosities and hostilities. This does not mean the offended takes a passive view on offences. Rather, the individual will select the best method for dealing with problems instead of resorting to a vengeful attitude towards infractions.

When we can release someone from a wrong that hurt us, we are not only helping that individual, but also building up our strength. In any case, forgiveness is really for the one who was hurt, which relieves him or her from the strain of emotional pain and being vengeful.

If we were to harbour hurts and resentment with a plan for future retaliation, we are only hurting ourselves and not the offender. However, the only way we can improve interpersonal relationships is by acknowledging that *we all make mistakes.*

Sin, which is selfish and destructive, is the major cause for all our pains, sicknesses, social and interpersonal conditions. Therefore, when there are problems in any situation, we must keep in mind that the enemy used someone who has responded to his schemes and plans against us to carry out that attack.

While we see the individual, we should recognize that this is a demonic attack even though humans are carrying out the deeds. Paul told us that we do not fight with flesh and blood, but against powers and spiritual forces (Ephesians 6:12).

When a disagreement occurs in a relationship, go to God in prayer to find out how to respond rather than react. He, through the Holy Spirit, will guide and direct you concerning what to do and how to respond. (Luke 18:1; I Peter 5:6-9).

What does Forgiveness Means?

Forgiveness will strengthen a relationship and build trust among persons. If there is no forgiveness social germs of resentment, bad attitudes, grudges, pride, and selfishness will develop and create conflict. In any case, if we do not treat others the way we want to be treated, animosities, hatred, and malice will take over. Do not allow an offense to cause you to live in misery by keeping it fresh on your mind. This does not mean you should or can forget the incident, but you must purpose in your heart not to hold a grudge against an offender. Forgiveness means you are emotionally releasing the offender from the hold he or she has on you, and you will feel much better.

1. *To forgive* someone does not mean you will forget the wrong done to you. Instead, it means that you are willing to overlook the fault. As time goes by you will find that the hurt gets less intense, and you can move on and pass that incident.

2. *To forgive* means you will no longer hold a grudge against the offender. Therefore, conflict will cease since there will be no cause for further dispute.

3. *To forgive* means you will look deep into your heart, and empty yourself of the effects of hurt from an offense and move forward (I Peter 5:7). Cast them on the Lord. The longer you hold on to a grudge the harder it will be to forgive. Furthermore, you will only keep yourself emotionally attached to the offender with the constant memory of the hurt.

Who Needs Forgiveness?

1. First, forgive *yourself* for any negative way you acted to cause discomfort for another.
2. Second, forgive *the person* who caused distress in your life.
3. Finally, forgive *God* because there are times when we blame Him for things which happen to us.

Points to think about (See Romans 12:9-21)

1. Relieve yourself of hurts, and do not seek for vengeance.
2. When you release the hurt, it will no longer have power over you.
3. Assume your responsibility in every situation.
4. Consider the consequences of an unforgiving attitude. The only person who hurts is you who refuses to forgive.
5. Never neglect to do that which is right and fair.
6. Be proactive in seeking reconciliation.
7. Avoid making excuses to clear you from the wrongs you have committed. Admit to your faults and shake off guilt and hurts.

Matthew 6:14-15

For if ye forgive men their trespasses,
your heavenly Father will also forgive you:

But if ye forgive not men their trespasses,
neither will your Father forgive your trespasses.

Exercises

The Meeting

Pappine arrived at 6:30 pm for the meeting to arrange a field trip for the group, scheduled to begin at 6:00 pm, but as was her habit, she was late again. The room was hot and uncomfortable for the ten persons gathered there. The air conditioning was broken, and the fans were doing their best to accommodate.

Mary looked over at Mackie who was playing his iPod, not caring about those present. She shouted at him to turn down the music. She was senior to him and always showed who was in charge when Pappine was absent.

Juarez a quiet guy, decided that he would not get into the battle, but he was sweating because the two students were getting out of control, added to the discomfort in the room. He thought that any minute they would come to blows being in each other's face.

Although Pappine had the tendency to be late, she knows how to calm a situation that could get out of hand. Her entrance was timely. She asked Mackie to turn off the music or listen through the headphones to avoid disturbing anyone. She then proceeded to comfort Judy who agreed that she had no offense against Mackie or his music.

The main irritation was the heat and discomfort in the small room. Things settled down and the meeting began with no further interruptions.

Analyze each Conflict Scenario for symptoms of

  i. Emotions

  ii. Blame

  iii. Psychological factors

  iv. Power Play

  v. Assertiveness/Aggressiveness

  vi. Accommodation

  vii. Interpersonal conflict

  viii. Intrapsychic conflict or dissonance

  ix. Fighting

  x. Compromising

  xi. Collaboration

  xii. Competitiveness

  xiii. Empathy

  xiv. Reflection

  xv. Avoidance

  xvi. Effective interpersonal communication

  xvii. Conflict management skills

  xviii. Destructive or constructive conflict elements

Melissa and Ginger

These two girls have been close friends for a long time. Recently Melissa questioned if Ginger is the right person to be with since she is so critical. Listen to the conversation below, and then discuss.

Melissa to Ginger
"I heard that *Frank* and *Challis* broke up."

Ginger. Phew, "I am not surprised. *Chuckle*, with a face like his, he should have stayed with *Challis*. Who else will have him?"

Melissa,
"That is so mean, Frank is our friend."
She thought about the remark and confronted Ginger.

Melissa to Ginger,

"That was unkind. You should not have said that about Frank.
Ginger, "*You*, told me about it." "Maybe you want him for yourself. Aha, I see now. In any case, what do you want to do with someone like Frank – ugh"!
Melissa walked away feeling distressed and saddened because she likes both *Ginger* and Frank.

Valuable Instructions about Wisdom

Proverbs 4:5-9

Get wisdom, get understanding: forget (it) not; neither decline from the words of my mouth.

Forsake her not, and she shall preserve thee: love her, and she shall keep thee.

Wisdom (is) the principal thing; (therefore) get wisdom: and with all thy getting get understanding.

Exalt her, and she shall promote thee: she shall bring thee to honour, when thou dost embrace her.

She shall give to thine head an ornament of grace: a crown of glory shall she deliver to thee.

Managing Conflict

Think of any conflict situation you have encountered, and answer the following questions.

1. Knowing what you understand about conflict, how could you have changed the situation?
2. How did the conflict get started, and what was it about?
3. What part did you play in the situation?
4. How did you arrive at defining the main problem, and finding out the underlying ones?
5. What was your response to the situation? Were you proactive or reactive?
6. Did you attack the problem or the person in the dispute?
7. If the other person attacked you, what was your response?
8. What approach did you use to deal with the problem?
9. Would you use that same style again? Why, or why not?
10. Did the other person understand your point of view?
11. Did you understand the other person's point of view?
12. Did you understand the reasons for the conflict?
13. How was the dispute settled?
14. What did you learn from your handling of the situation?
15. Now that it is over, what would you have changed?

Personal Communication Style

		Yes	No
1.	I always make my objections known when I disagree with someone.	Yes	No
2.	I really do not take time to listen to the other person's point of view.		
3.	I try to listen to the other person by asking questions to gain understanding, and show respect.		
4.	I always try to check my body language to keep a balance.		
5.	I give up easily when I find that I am not being heard.		
6.	I say what I mean in a quiet way to avoid upsetting anyone.		
7.	I really do not care how others feel about me. I always please myself.		
8.	I am able to express my feelings better when I am angry because *everybody* listens when I am boiling.		
9.	I always care about how other people feel and therefore, I suppress my own feelings.		
10.	I keep the peace because I care very much about keeping relationships intact.		
11.	I easily get angry, and say things that I later regret		
12.	I am a very impatient person.		
13.	I do not care about other peoples' deficiencies. That is not my concern.		
14.	I remain silent, even to what is wrong.		
15.	I believe that everyone should be respected.		
16.	I am more interested in getting my point across.		

Adapted by B. Y. Stuart ©Copyright 2011

The Mediation Process

> **Mediator**
> This must be an objective person, who will show respect and regard for the disputants.

> **The Mediator facilitates Communication, and *Directs* the discussion.**
> He or she does not tell the parties what to do. Instead, the person listens, and maintain order while the parties discuss their disagreements. Resolution must be determined by the parties themselves, and confirmed by the mediator.

> **Agreement**
> The aim of the Mediator is to help the disputants reach an amicable resolution to their problems. As a facilitator, the person should obtain commitments from the disputants that they will stand by the agreements.

Adapted by B. Y. Stuart ©Copyright 2011

Conflict Management Styles
Assessment Work Sheet

<u>Scale</u>: *Strongly Agree* **SA**-5; *Agree* **A**-4; *Disagree* **D**-3;
Strongly Disagree **SD**-2; *Neutral* **N**-0.

CONFLICT STYLES	SA	A	D	SD	N
1. Avoidance I usually end a discussion quickly without discovering the reason for someone's unsociable behaviour.					
2. Compromise Although I knew the decision was against my better judgment, I allowed the other person's desire so that we would each be satisfied.					
3. Competitive In a conversation, I am happy when everyone accepts my suggestions, instead of anyone else's.					
4. Collaborative After listening and identifying concerns, usually I offer solutions that I believe could bring about an amicable outcome.					
5. Accommodation I always agree with other people, even if I know that something was against my beliefs and values.					

Scoring:

How did you score with items 1-3 and 5? If you scored higher with these Items than with item 4, you would need to evaluate your conflict resolution style. *Note: there will be times when you will have to use the best approach suitable for the situation. For example, you would not want to argue with someone who is angry and who might physically harm you.*

Adapted by B.Y. Stuart ©Copyright 2011

The Influence of Emotions in Conflict Situations

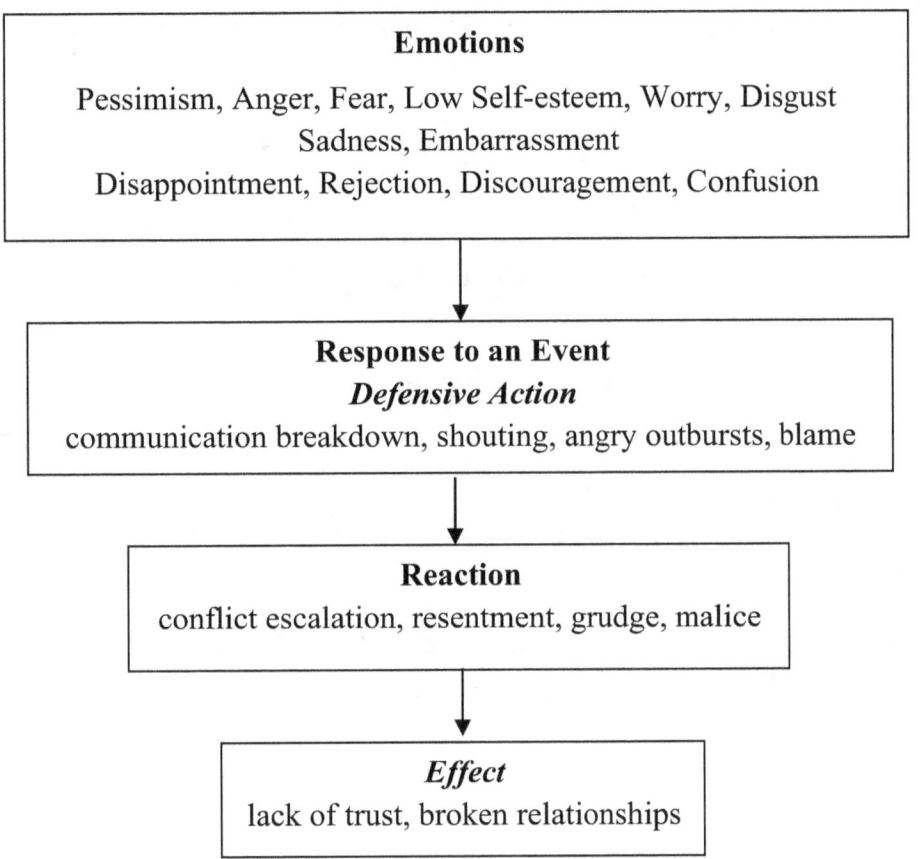

Emotions

Pessimism, Anger, Fear, Low Self-esteem, Worry, Disgust
Sadness, Embarrassment
Disappointment, Rejection, Discouragement, Confusion

Response to an Event
Defensive Action
communication breakdown, shouting, angry outbursts, blame

Reaction
conflict escalation, resentment, grudge, malice

Effect
lack of trust, broken relationships

Adapted by B. Y. Stuart ©Copyright 2011

Not every challenge is worth a confrontation.

Sometimes, *walk* away!

You will *not* be sorry you did.

Dare to be different!

If you *know* something is wrong,

don't do it!

Non-violent Exercises

There are many ways the youth can adopt to ward off conflict and prevent violence. The list below is only suggestions to help maintain peace and order.

1. Someone causes you to trip and spill your drink. Instead of saying, "You idiot didn't you see me coming?"
   Say, "I am sorry I was not looking where I was going."

2. If you caused the person to trip and spill the drink, own up and apologize with sincerity, rather than laugh.
   I am so sorry, let me help you clean up.

3. You were driving and minding your own business when someone cuts across you with no signal. It made you become agitated and almost caused an accident.
   Instead of cursing and using negative body language, let the driver go and do not act aggressively by speeding up to get even.
   Always choose the peaceful path to prevent escalation of conflict.
   Furthermore, it is better to wait one minute to let the other person go, than to wait for the police if there is an accident or physical altercation. Keep the consequences for your action in focus.

4. You got on the school bus, and everyone laughed at you for no apparent reason. While passing by Jim, he touched his friend Janice and they both snickered.
   There is no need to start a fight with words or get physical. You could ask if there is something wrong. Maybe check yourself to see if something is unusual about your dressing. If you are comfortable, ignore the behaviour of the other person. Silence to an instigator goes deeper than you could ever imagine. You do not have to respond with violence.

5. The next morning Jim purposely stands by the locker door, blocking you.

    Instead of shoving your way through, say, "Excuse me" and wait for him to remove himself. He may have planned an attack when he saw you coming. Give him the element of surprise by not reacting to his plan.

6. You arrived at school and found a troublesome student sitting in your usual place. There are other empty tables where you can sit.

    You said to the student "This is where I usually sit, please find another place." This is someone who is about your size and you could take him on in a fight. He says to you "I am taking this seat, what are you going to do about it?"

    Calmly say to him, there is no need to act this way. You normally sit over there, and I sit here. If he continues to be belligerent, just move away and let him have the seat.

    Why would you want to tarnish your conduct by inciting a fight only for a seat? Always think about consequences before acting aggressively.

7. *Alice and Mary* do not get along. *Alice* picks on her and constantly criticizes her about her appearance and dressing. For a long time, she has been inciting a confrontation. One afternoon, while *Mary* waited for her mom at the bus stop, *Alice* appeared with one of her friends.

    Mary's best friend *Charlie* who rides with her was waiting there too. When *Alice* saw *Mary*, she sneered and brushed against her shoulder. *Charlie* was annoyed and asked, "Are you going to take that from her. She disrespected you. Get in her face and show that you are not afraid?"

In such a situation, it would be easy for Mary to respond to the urging of her friend Charlie to save face.

However, one solution to this is to ignore Alice's behaviour and wait for a convenient time to approach her concerning the dispute between them.

Another response could be for Mary to say, "Alice did you notice that you bounced me without saying sorry?"

If she speaks quietly without animosity, Mary might get the attention of the offender.

To react otherwise, it might only escalate the situation and cause more problems.

Anger will lead you into

an *emotional*

quicksand.

Pause,

before accepting that

challenge to do

what is wrong or to fight.

Suggestions for Confrontation

1. <u>Do not blame</u>: Avoid pointing fingers, blaming, or getting into the other person's face with the use of "*you...*"

   Instead of saying, *"You disrespected me; what is wrong with you?"*
   <u>Say in a quiet non-hostile manner</u>, *"I am not sure what has happened, but did I do something to you?*

2. <u>Give the other person an opportunity to explain</u>. When you approach in a non-violent manner, this will take the aggressor by surprise because he or she is expecting a fight.

3. <u>A soft word will work better than insults</u>. If you have been insulted, it hurts. Nevertheless, if you are the better person, let your behaviour represent who you are and what you believe, rather than act on impulse to prove yourself or save face. Sometimes, a smile, walking away, and silence are great for preventing violence that could escalate into physical encounters.

4. <u>Choose a private place for discussion</u>. Do not confront in the presence of others if you feel safe talking one on one with the individual in private. No one else needs to hear what you are saying. Always put yourself in the other person's shoe.

5. <u>Facing hostilities from the offender</u>: If the person who insulted you continues with disrespect when you are trying to resolve the situation, then call someone to be present to avoid any physical encounter by either of you. It is better to be safe than sorry.

6. <u>Name-calling</u>: The person may call you a nasty name, which makes you feel embarrassed, especially when others are listening. Do not cause more shame to yourself by approaching that person or using foul language.

Whatever comes out of your mouth tells others who you are. Your behaviour describes your character.

In such a situation, sometimes just shaking your head, ignoring, and walking away in silence will work wonders. The instigator will end up being ashamed because you did not respond to cause embarrassment.

7. <u>Facing Blame</u>: People often blame others for their own faults because they refuse to own up to their weaknesses. If you have to confront someone about something he or she did but blamed you, do not to use direct language.

   Ask, "*Do you know who did...*" and wait for the response. Give the person the opportunity to own up to faults. When there is refusal, then you can present proof in a calm and quiet manner without accusation.

Wherefore, my beloved brethren, let every man be
swift to hear, slow to speak, slow to wrath:
(James 1: 19)